Feeling My Emotions

By H. J. Ray

Text and illustrations Copyright 2023. All Rights Reserved.
Published by My Wellbeing School Press.

*You are a ray of light,
filled with color, shining bright.
If sometimes your light feels dim,
remember you have a rainbow within.*

When I feel blue,

I try to feel yellow.

When I feel red,

I try to feel pink.

When I feel green,

I try to feel gold.

When I feel gray,

I try to feel orange.

If I let those colors
be heard and seen,
the feelings inside them
wash away clean.

It's OK to feel

all the colors.

So if pink turns to red
or yellow to blue,

I won't be afraid.
I'll know what to do.

I'll sit with the color.

I'll listen, maybe we'll go for a walk.

And when we're outside in the light of day, I can hear what my color's been trying to say.

Then I put down the color,
say "thank you for sharing",
and reach for the color
I'd rather be wearing.

When my colors are heard, I feel lighter and free to sparkle with my favorite colors in me.

Sometimes, finding the right words to express our emotions can be difficult. It takes practice to understand our feelings and communicate them with others.

Coming up are the mood pages again. Take a look at the pictures and see what words you can come up with to describe the feelings.

upset

rejected

drained

down

unhappy

sad

blue

lonely

hurt

disappointed

hopeless

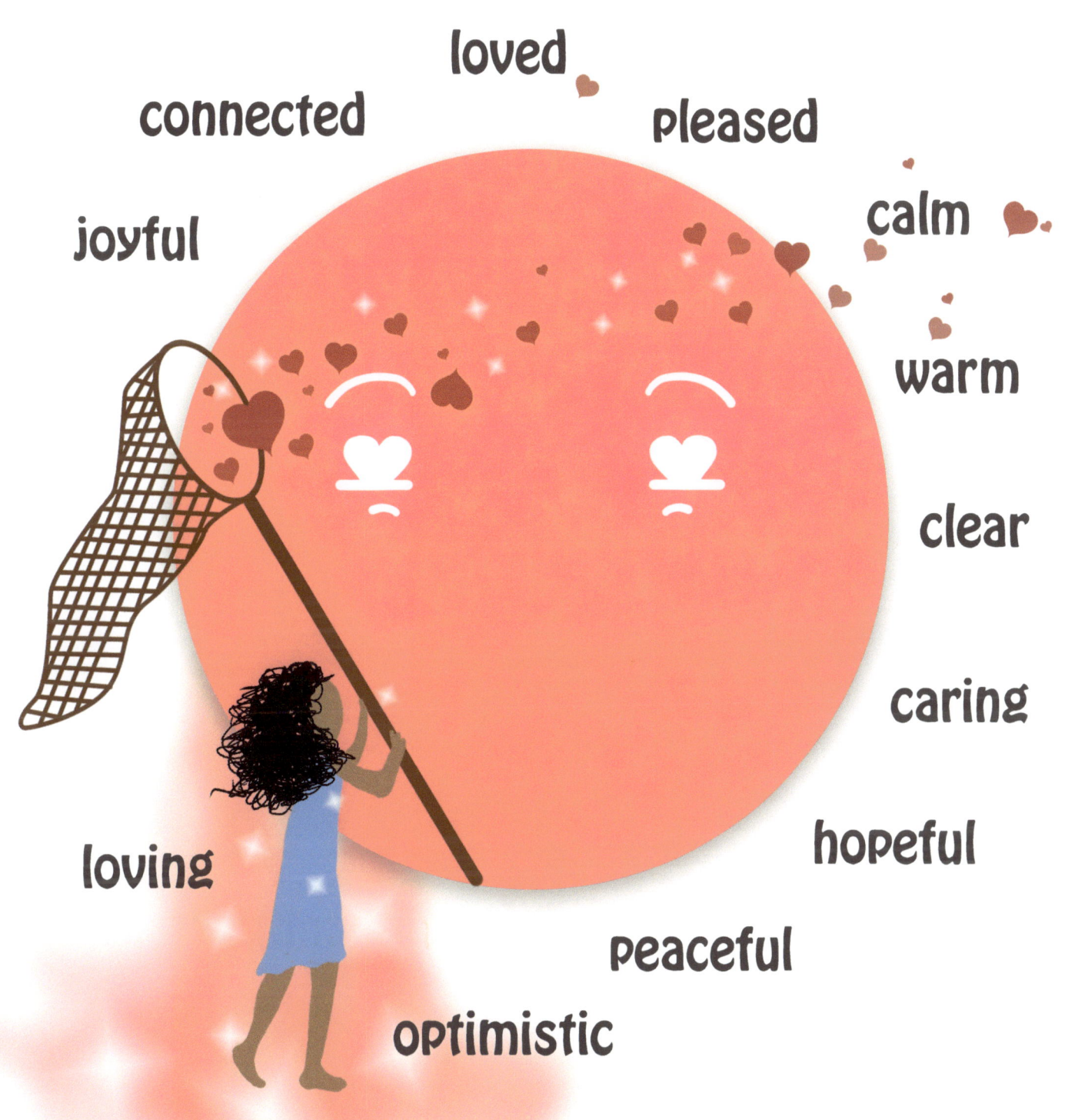

suspicious

frustrated

resentful

nervous

envious

selfish

jealous

annoyed

confused

worried

uncomfortable

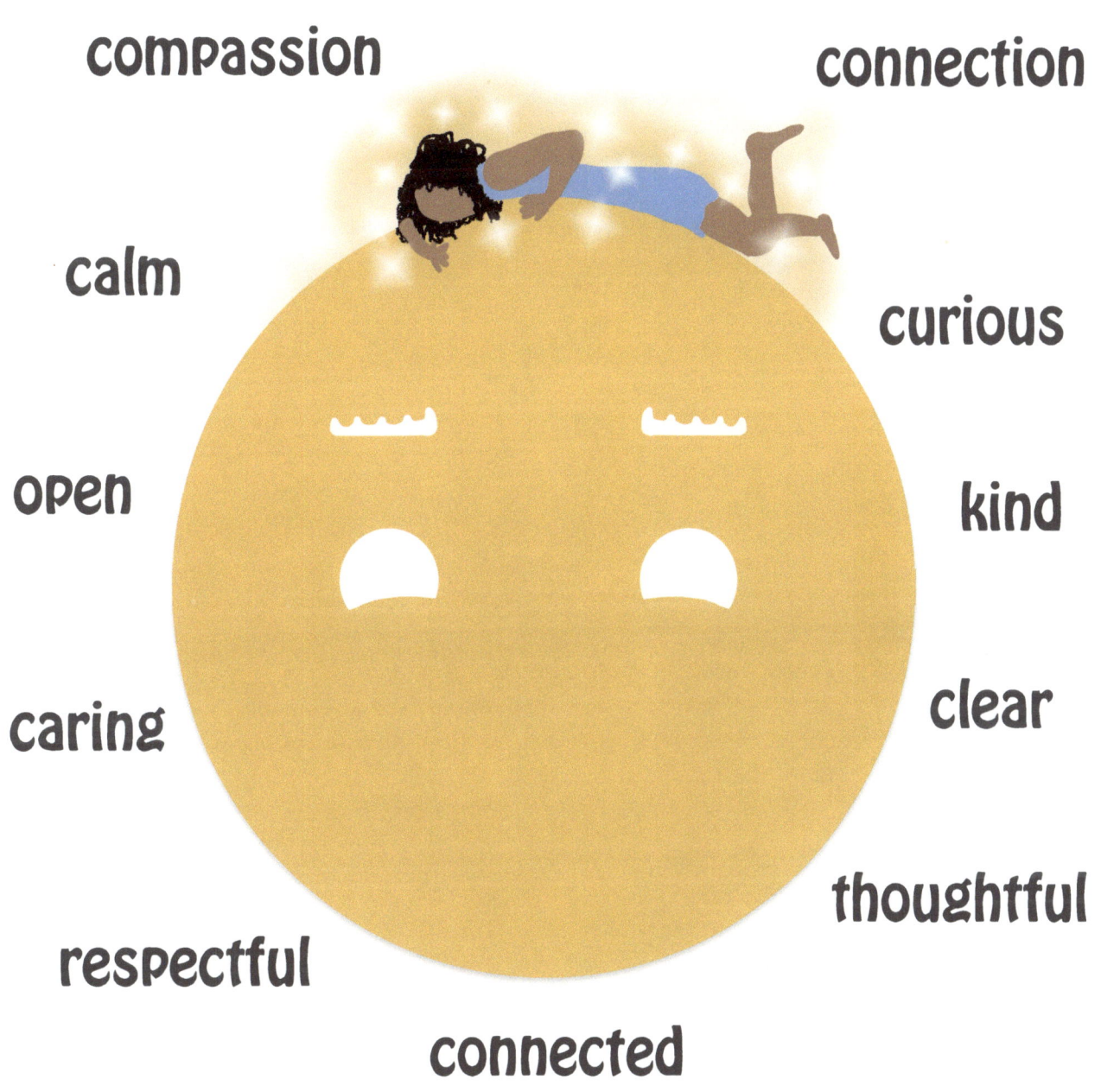

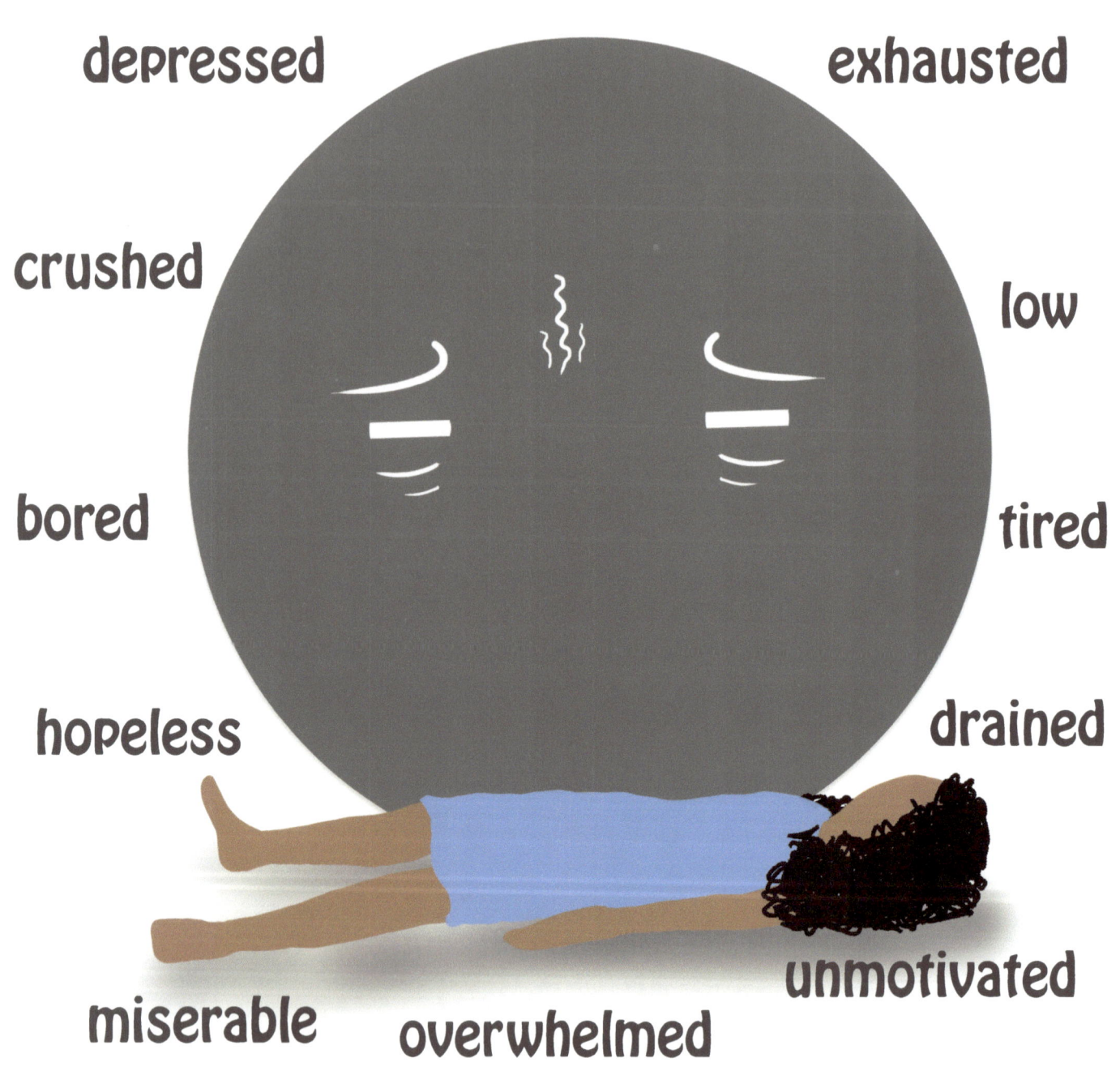

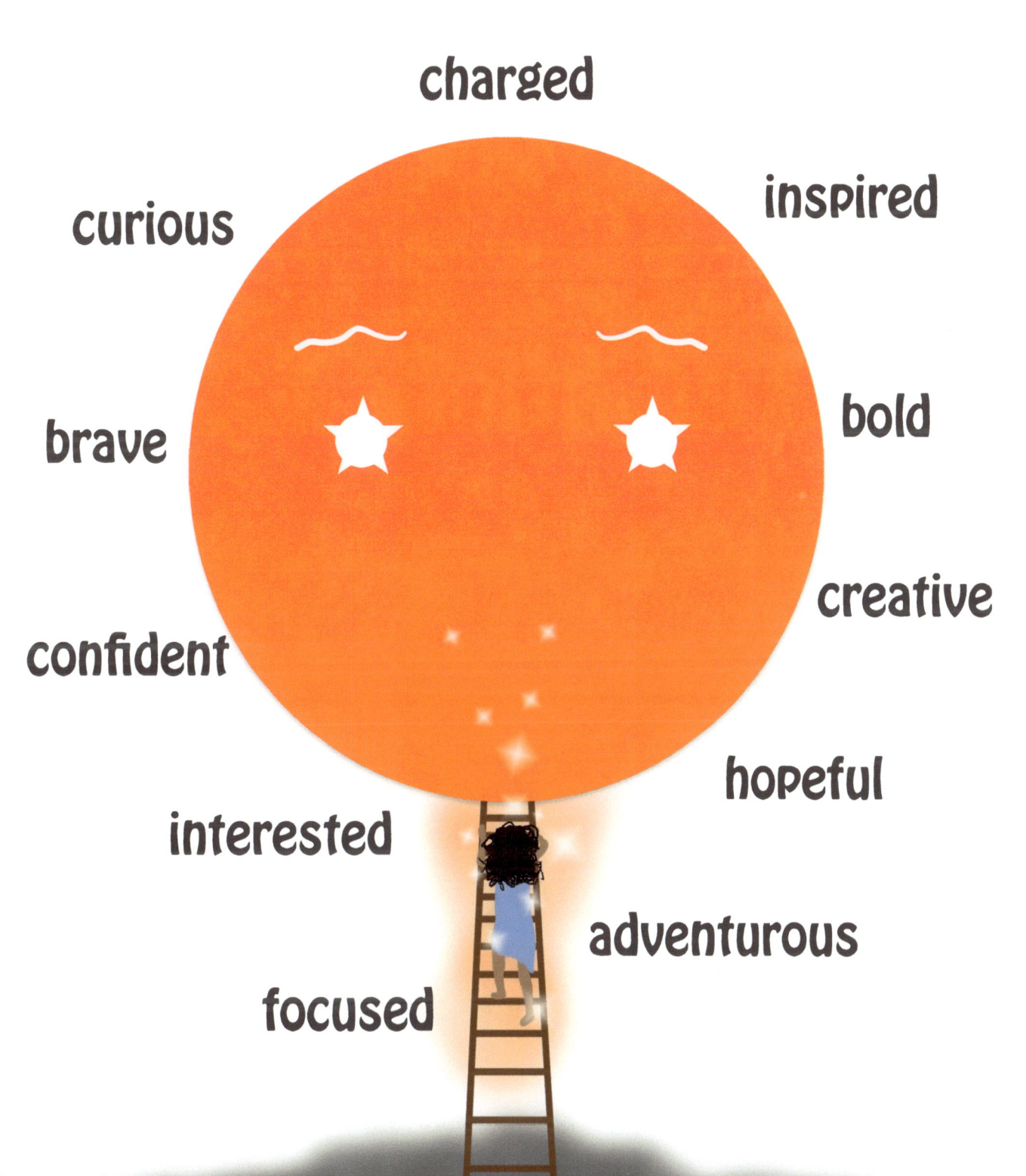

How do you think colors are related to emotions?

Do you think everyone feels emotions in the same way?

Let's explore hidden depths

This is called holding space for your feelings.

Our character is observing their feelings to understand what they are trying to say.

Sometimes, emotions can be so strong that it's hard to think clearly, or we can feel a mixture of so many different emotions that it can feel like a puzzle we have to work out.

The more practice we have in understanding our feelings, the better we get at choosing to feel good.

Notice how our character is always in active pursuit of good feelings.

Holding on to happiness,

trying to catch love,

reaching for compassion,

or climbing to courage.

Feeling good is a choice that requires action!

Lying on the ground and feeling disappointed is fine. Feeling that disappointment is important.

But when you are ready to feel hopeful, you have to pull yourself up and do something.

What helps you to feel happy?

In your opinion, what's happening in this sequence?

Our character is holding space for the emotion they are feeling, which appears to be anger. But there is more going on beneath the surface.

Often, love or wounded love hides behind anger. Part of holding space for our emotions is not to judge how we are feeling but to allow those feelings to come up so we can let them go.

I have created a great meditation you can access via the link in this book to help you with this process.

Thank you for sharing!

You are not your feelings. Feelings are like visitors in your home. Treat them kindly, listen to them, say "thank you for sharing," and then take action from your powerful, loving, hopeful state.

Keep the conversation going...

Head over to www.mywellbeingschool.com/wordsgift and download your special bonus gift pack.

Feeling My Emotions By H. J. Ray

Guided Meditation

Words For My Feelings

Printables for your home or classroom

MORE BOOKS BY H. J. RAY

Heather Ray is an author/illustrator and wellbeing program designer. Heather studied Applied Theatre and Education at the Royal Central School of Speech and Drama, where her taste for education took off. She later qualified as a Body Control Pilates Instructor, moved to Hong Kong to study Chinese Kung Fu, and co-founded a Health and Wellbeing Club in the City Centre in 2008. In 2013, Heather moved to Cyprus to study psychotherapy and meditation with a spiritual group called the Researchers of Truth. There, her work became more focused on counselling, healing, and meditation. In 2017, Heather moved to Australia, where she now calls home, and founded My Wellbeing School. Heather's flare for creativity, design, wealth of wellbeing expertise, and relatable character make her programs engaging and irresistible to families, schools, and therapists alike.

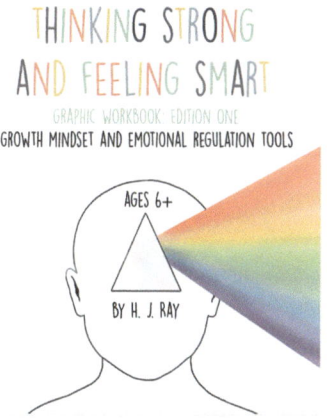

For more information, to book an event, workshop or to enquire about coaching programs, email
info@mywellbeingschool.com

www.ingramcontent.com/pod-product-compliance
Lightning Source LLC
Chambersburg PA
CBHW041427010526
44107CB00045B/1530